100 Things

Every College Freshman Ought to Know

An abridged college orientation catalog of definitions, customs, procedures, and plain old good advice about adjusting to the start of college.

by William Disbro

Cambridge Stratford Study Skills Institute
Williamsville, New York

100 Things Every College Freshman Ought to Know
by William Disbro

Copyright © 1995
The Cambridge Stratford Study Skills Institute
A division of Cambridge Stratford, Ltd.
8560 Main Street, Williamsville, New York 14221.
For information: (716) 626-9044.

The
Cambridge
Stratford
Study Skills
Institute™

Library of Congress Number: 95-067191
ISBN: 0-935637-22-2   Printed in the USA
Printing is the lowest number: 20 19 18 17 16 15 14 13

Icons and drawings by
William Disbro

Acknowledgements

The author wishes to acknowledge the many colleagues, students and families who have provided suggestions and experiences that seem important in pursuing success in college. In addition, two college interns were employed by the publisher to review, edit, and improve specific parts. Many thanks to Ms. Amanda Campagna, State University of New York at Buffalo, and Andrew Lucyszyn, St. Bonaventure University, for their tireless efforts in helping to develop the book from the student's perspective. Sincere appreciation also to Shelley Grice for her proofreading. This art professor has needed much help through the years and Shelley has been terrific! Thank you all!

Who is the Author?

A college instructor for over twenty-five years and currently a Professor of Art at Jamestown Community College, I'm mid-fifties in age with three children who have all achieved bachelor's degrees. My wife has been a part-time art instructor at my college for fifteen years. Together we have had lots of experience with college environments and situations, both from instructors' viewpoints and from being college parents. Also, remember that I was once a college student, something that students find hard to believe.

My three children would tell you that growing up in a home with artist parents is not all fun. One artist living with another is not always harmonious — look at van Gogh and Gauguin. There were times when the living room was used as a studio to house large steel and ceramic sculpture pieces in progress of fabrication. However, the children survived, made their parents proud, graduated from colleges and moved on with their lives leaving many good memories of living with artist/parents. Also, they left us useful information to share with others beginning the college experience. Their experiences and those of my students who all dealt with the somewhat frustrating and anxious adjustment to becoming a college freshman have provided the core of issues to be listed in this offering of advice. Life is full of choices. The more you know, the better your decisions will be. Good luck!

Photo by Tobin Disbro

Your first lesson in college is that almost no professor will
be able to finish on time. You will be receiving more
information than you bargained for— as in this book,
there are more than 100 things . . .

Work hard - you can never waste your time in learning.

Introduction

Stop! Read this before going forward.

This line should be printed at the beginning of every introduction of freshmen textbooks. Why? Because many freshmen don't read introductions to books. Many jump right into the "important" stuff. The result is they miss some *real* important stuff; things like the book's theme, and the tone and goals of the author. Also, many times the purpose is clearly stated in the introduction and gives relevancy to your reason for reading. So consider this one of those "100 things you should know." Read introductions!

My purpose in writing this book is to share some key items that may help you adjust to your first year in college — items that you may not get from your college catalog — items that will help make your college catalog more understandable.

The need for this book evolved from my experience as a college art instructor but hit home about 1987 when my daughter asked a question about something I thought should have been covered in the college catalog. When I asked if she had read the catalog, she responded, "You've got to be kidding Dad, you need a Ph.D. to understand it." Not to be proven wrong, I tried to help her find the information in her catalog. I failed in my attempt. Many of the items she needed were not included and those covered were difficult to read, used vocabulary unique to colleges, and required a knowledge of the structure and organization of the college setting to understand. I made a list of her concerns and asked a classroom of new freshmen to add to it. The list grew. By 1993, I offered a suggestion to my community college: Keep the college catalog as it is but let me write an abridged college orientation catalog that included many of these issues. I did. It was printed in 1994 and circulated to our freshmen. That began a wave of other suggestions and helpful hints from students, faculty, and parents that indicated a tremendous need for wider circulation of a book of this type. *100 Things* is the result.

Your reading of this book will give you the awareness that hundreds of students before you have discovered is important in adjusting to college. Some items will be easy to handle and others will require further investigation, research, and thought. Your own college catalog will probably seem clearer to you after your reading and should be used for further research.

This is the beginning of a big step in your life. Realize you are not alone. This book will help you open discussions with your friends, instructors, and parents. Their insights will further heighten your awareness. Possibly, your college or high school will use this text in a seminar or discussion group to explore key points more fully. Know as much as possible as you take this step and rely on those around you to help.

My second message deals with the style, tone, and layout of this book. The layout is designed to be creative and enjoyable, not sequential in importance. As an art professor, I call this design eclectic. Much of your college experience will be eclectic as well. You won't experience it in an orderly fashion. However, should you wish to locate information in an orderly fashion, an index is provided. Topics are generally categorized but many overlap and intertwine. As you read *100 Things* please don't be offended by my writing something that is already well known to you. Student reviews of this material have shown that some students would omit many specific items because they are so obvious, yet others say the same items are informative and must be retained. So what's an art professor to do? I left the items in. Read them all. Make a visual experience out of this: take dark-colored markers and cover over items you find unnecessary or already known, then take bright colored markers and highlight the most important items (a good study skills technique). Anyway, after you've marked the material, you'll probably feel ownership of hopefully some helpful suggestions. In sum, heightened interest and easy reading are my goals in using the tone and style I chose. Hope you agree.

IMPORTANT – Don't stop yet.

My final message is my goal to make this book even more helpful to future students. Like making a collage of visual bits and pieces, this book has grown out of the ideas of others. It's title, *100 Things*, can grow to a new edition of *200 Things* with your help. I'd like to include a reference of individual contributors in my next edition. If you'll send a statement about a topic you feel should be covered, I'll include your name, institution, and status (student, faculty, parent, etc.) as a credit for your contribution. A form is included on page 187. As you read, jot down your ideas on the appropriate page. When you've finished, transfer your ideas to this form, fill in the biographical information, and return to the address listed. This way, you'll receive a by-line for your editorial contribution and assist the next incoming class of freshmen to make a smoother transition to college. Thank you in advance, Henry David Thoreaus of the world.

Now, go forward. Sit back (i.e., under a tree, at McDonald's, at a peaceful lake, or in the solitude of your own room) and let's explore college from an artistic perspective . . . a little here, a little there. Read with purpose, an understanding of style, and try out the role of book editor by sharing your thoughts. I'd love to hear from you.

William Disbro, 1995

Table of Contents

SUNDAY	MONDAY	TUESDAY	WEDNESDAY	T
Sleep 'til noon	Help Ralph with car until pool time	Up by noon — eat	2 for 1 game day in Union	S u
Eat	Eat	Cheap film day downtown	Party in 212	R
Touch Football afternoon	Party at Frat House	Party at Bob's	Party at Arlene's sister's	Pa #3
Party at Jen's				

Scheduling disaster.

Behaviors

to be encouraged and avoided

College Freshmen Ought to Know:

1.   that it is important to **read introductions** in this and every book in college. They often state the purpose for your reading. Did you read the introduction to this book? If not, return to page vii and do so now. Also, if you're thinking you'll go back and do it later, you're practicing **procrastination**. It's a killer of college students. Studies indicate the first six weeks of the first term of college are crucial to student decisions to stay or leave college. If you're a would-be procrastinator, become pro-active immediately. Set goals, do first things first (as in reading the introduction and finishing this book) and stop dreaming about how you'll look in that cap and gown on graduation day. The moment is now to work towards that goal.

College Freshmen Ought to Know:

2.   that **college is very different** from high school.   In high school almost everything you did was planned by someone else: the courses, your schedule of classes, your readings, your meals, etc.   In college — you're on your own.   You have complete freedom to become successful in your life — or you can fail out, all by yourself.   For better or for worse, in college and life, it's all up to you.

College Freshmen Ought to Know:

3.   that it is your **responsibility to question**. Question everything, assume nothing. Start with, "Why am I here?" (Where are you?) Be alert in situations where people are anxious to change something. You ought to ask, "Who benefits?" In examining any situation, from business market arrangements to psychological behavior to analysis of hours of operation of the library or student union, ask who is benefiting from the the situation? It may be merely interesting to find

out why things operate the way they do, but if you want to change anything you must find out how to show people that your proposals will help them. If you can't show an improvement you probably will not be successful in significantly changing anything. This is not just about college operation hours, it's also about national tariff restrictions, union negotiations, race relations, etc.

College Freshmen Ought to Know:

4.   that another **change from high school** is the **diversity of students** that you will meet. Whereas in high school the similarities of students far outweighed the differences among students, in college you will have a variety of ages, races, backgrounds, beliefs, experiences, interests, and especially abilities sitting next to you in class. College is an atmosphere of intelligence and learning. Don't close yourself off from experiences with any of these students. That is the world coming to learn and you are a part of that world.

College Freshmen Ought to Know:

5.   never to **misspell** the instructor's name. Nothing signals sloppy, lazy ineptitude to the instructor as much as when a student can't even get his/her name correctly spelled.

College Freshmen Ought to Know:

6.   **never to begin a conversation** with a faculty member by saying, "I've tried to find you many times but you are never here . . ." If the faculty member truly never is on campus — he/she doesn't want to be reminded by a student. But, more often than not, faculty members spend most of their days on campus; you just need to know where to look. Find their secretaries and get a schedule of the office

hours, or set up an appointment to meet with the faculty member; post notes on his/her office door. Also, check out where the faculty member spends time; this is a great opportunity to find out what a real laboratory or studio or research facility looks like. Be persistent.

College Freshmen Ought to Know:

7. **how to address instructors**. Some instructors prefer to be formal, others are comfortable on a first name basis. Let the instructor set the tone. If no address is offered, ask instructors how they wished to be addressed. If you do not know, always err on the side of formality, as in Professor so-and-so, or Dr. so-and-so. Just like everywhere else, flattery will get you everywhere.

College Freshmen Ought to Know:

8.   to be **polite in relations** with faculty members. Like it or not the ultimate power resides with the grade giver. Be very polite, but persistent. Don't be afraid to ask questions — the same question again if necessary. If you can engage humor it will always be welcomed — but never at the instructor's expense. Remember, any positive feelings between you and your instructor can only benefit you as a student.

College Freshmen Ought to Know:

9.   that you must **treat custodians and secretaries with great respect**. These people may save your soul someday by preventing a personal disaster for you. Custodians can find jumper cables to start dead car batteries and they have keys that can get you into an area that they don't really have to open for you — or even shouldn't open for you — like a lab or studio to let you work after hours. Secretaries can find faculty members to sign forms when faculty don't want to be found. Good secretaries really know what's happening in the department; in fact, a lot of secretaries know more about how departments operate than the department heads.

College Freshmen Ought to Know:

10.   that in some college situations the **competition among students** is so fierce that unattended book bags will be taken, not for money, but for good class notes. An entire course or even all work for all courses can disappear from a study table in only the time it takes to go to the rest room.

College Freshmen Ought to Know:

11. that **parties, drinking, and late hours** will take a toll on your body no matter how young and virile you are. Sooner or later it will catch up with you, and you will not have the time or the concentration necessary to do the required coursework, which your grades will reflect. Some fun is good, even necessary to break up the routine of study, but keep Ben Franklin in mind: moderation in all things . . .

College Freshmen Ought to Know:

12. the importance of the **first class meeting**. The first class meeting sets the tone for the entire term. The entire course is laid out: what it's all about, what is required of students, when papers are due, what the assigned readings are, and what is and is not acceptable behavior. Handout sheets will be distributed. Don't miss the first meeting. Some instructors accomplish nothing and only make a joke of the first meeting. But that is their choice. **You** should be ready for serious stuff because some instructors *are* ready to start. Well-prepared, conscientious instructors also know the importance of that first meeting. You may be conspicuous by your absence and set a tone with your instructor that may be hard to overcome.

College Freshmen Ought to Know:

13. that **attendance** in class must be carefully considered. Know what your instructor desires. Some do not take attendance, some will. Some do not care if you ever attend their class, some want you there every single time. Know what it takes to be successful in that class. Most classes require constant attendance simply to get the material. Sometimes material presented in lecture is not found in the textbooks and it's up to you to find out if that material will be on the exams; ask

people who have taken the course, look at old exams. In courses with required attendance, if you miss a class, a note from your mother won't help you. At least one college has a policy that if three classes are missed, for any reason, the student must withdraw from that class or fail the course! Be sure to know the instructor's attendance policy for every class you take.

College Freshmen Ought to Know:

14.   that being **late to class** can be embarrassing. In some classes the door is locked when the lecture begins, in other classes the instructor will use you to illustrate particular behavior as he/she asks you questions while you try to disappear into a seat. In other classes nobody will know or even care if you are late or not there. Again, it comes down to you deciding what you want to get out of this experience — you've paid for it. In some classes with rigid attendance policies, missing a class the last meeting before a vacation or the first meeting after a vacation will count as a double-cut.

On the other hand, how long do you wait for the instructor? Traditionally, students have been expected to sit in a classroom and wait for the instructor using a standard, yet unwritten rule:

Instructor - 5 min.

Assistant Professor - 10 min.

Associate Professor - 15 min.

Professor - 20 min.

Usually, if the instructor knows he/she will be late or absent, someone will come to tell the assembled class. Err by waiting and use the time to review your notes.

College Freshmen Ought to Know:

15. it is important **to take part in activities on campus**. Of course there is so much going on all the time you must pick and choose, but get involved in things that interest you, and even things that you know nothing about. Some of those unknown clubs and activities might very well be the start of something very important in your life. Accept some responsibility at your first meeting. You will quickly learn if you can contribute something to the group. It's more fun to be involved. You'll know what's going on and you'll feel more at home in your college setting. Don't zoom off campus after class or spend every weekend at the local pizzaria with old friends. Stay on campus,

get involved and make some new friends!

Also, don't be afraid to start a new club or organization. The fact that your college doesn't offer something doesn't mean it can't. Take the initiative. It will be a great experience and one you can enjoy as an outcome of your own efforts.

The message here is to be part of out-of-class activities. It's part of the wider opportunity for learning on your campus (i.e., cooperation, goal setting, time on task, planning, etc.).

College Freshmen Ought to Know:

16. never to **mix colors** when doing the laundry.[1]

[1] Suggestion from Ms. Kathleen Hodges, Assistant Professor, Business, Jamestown Community College, Cattaraugus County Campus, 1993.

College Freshmen Ought to Know:

17. that they must be willing to **ask for help** as soon as they think they need it. The very first person to ask — not the last — is the instructor. Most faculty want students to succeed. Don't ever be embarrassed about discussing any problem affecting that course. Let the instructor know why you miss a class or if you have difficulty seeing or hearing. Ask for advice and do so early. You cannot make up an entire term's worth of material in the last week of classes. Also, the Learning Assistance Center is another outlet. It has a range of support services that can really help.

College Freshmen Ought to Know:

18. about **time management**. Students who organize their time and stick to a schedule normally do better than those that don't. There are a wide variety of time management approaches from which to choose. You may need to change the form you used in high school to operate effectively in college. Be prepared! It's a natural evolution to the college process. Try an approach. For example, have a system of folders and notebooks for each class. Take your academic calendar and break it down into weeks. List major events first, (i.e., mid-terms, finals, due dates for papers, etc.). Next, take the first week and sched-

ule everything you think will happen: sleeping, eating, work, classes, play time, and the one thing a lot of students forget to build into their schedule, study time. Two hours of study time (i.e., reading, reviewing notes, etc.) should be scheduled for each hour in class although some classes will not require all that time and some will require much more. Keep adjusting until you find the approach that works best for you. Keep this motto in mind as you proceed:

Plan Your Work, Then Work Your Plan.

College Freshmen Ought to Know:

19. that forming a **study group** with fellow students (same lecture/ lab session) is an excellent way to prepare for exams. This is a serious group — not a party. Select members carefully. All members should be willing to work. If not, dump them. Form the group by writing a note on the board for interested people to decide when and where to meet. No more than four to six people. Form study groups early in the term to assign responsibilities for collecting materials. Meet as often as necessary to ensure everyone is doing his/her share and to exchange materials. Faculty try to encourage study groups because they are effective methods of learning the material. Some faculty will even help set up study groups. Just keep the groups serious and stick to the subject to make them productive.

College Freshmen Ought to Know:

20. that successful students realize the importance of keeping themselves informed about **what is happening in the rest of the world**. Get into the habit of reading a newspaper daily. Not just one section, skim the entire paper. Select a good paper; the *USA TODAY* is sometimes called the "comic paper" for its lack of depth but full color approach — however, it does give a survey of news — and it's available! If not a daily newspaper, at least read a weekly news magazine. Faculty members will always assume you are keeping up on world events, often relating their material to world events. This is a good habit to pick up; once you start you'll get hooked on information.

College Freshmen Ought to Know:

21. that **faculty are very serious** about their academic disciplines. Whatever their field, it has become a major portion of their lives and they love it. They are excited when their enthusiasm rubs off onto students. If you are truly interested in what they are doing in their own research or creative production, don't be afraid to ask them about it. They will enjoy any discussion about what is so near and dear to them. This is also a great way for you to learn about the material and how it relates to the rest of the world. Occasionally a faculty member will ask for assistance with a project. This is a great opportunity to get involved in the field and learn more about how it works. These opportunities will be good items to list on your resume but also may give you suggestions about further study and career possibilities.

College Freshmen Ought to Know:

22. to **take seriousness seriously**. All of college life is not serious, but some of it is. Be able to bring problem solving, goal setting, critical thinking to the moment when needed. Save the play time and fun and games for appropriate places. If you work hard you can play hard.

College Freshmen Ought to Know:

23. that whatever **out-of-class obligations** you will have, your first priority is course grades. If you are playing sports you must be able to keep enough quality time for your studies or you are really fooling yourself on why you are attending college. How many basketball players start careers in college basketball and end up with multi-million dollar contracts in the NBA? Very few. Most employment interviewers really don't care whether or not you played ball; they want to know what you can do for them. Additionally, when planning your schedule of all the things that must be done on a weekly basis (time

management), students are usually advised not to work more than 15 hours a week. If you can't financially survive on 15 hours a week and must increase the work hours, perhaps you aren't ready for college at this time. Maybe you ought to work for as many hours as you can get for a term or two, save as much money as you can, and then go to college. Don't try to work full-time and go to college full-time. About halfway through the term you will find you are not successful at college and probably aren't very successful at work either. You can't do both and really gain value — nobody can.

Personal Suggestions
to help make the transition to college life

College Freshmen Ought to Know:

24.   to **flush**. Nobody wants to walk into the rest room and clean up after you.

College Freshmen Ought to Know:

25.   that in **packing** to go off to college you should lay everything out on the floor that you intend to pack. Now eliminate one half of all that stuff and you'll be about right. Students traveling to college for the first time usually take much more than they really need, particularly things like books, personal articles (stuffed animals), and even clothing. Take care not to overlook items such as electrical outlet strips, a screwdriver, a can opener, etc. Although these may not occur to you when you first pack, you'll be surprised by how often you'll need them and by how few people have them. Rest assured, each year you return to college you will have a clearer idea of what to bring. Things forgotten can always be shipped later!

College Freshmen Ought to Know:

26. that you need to watch your **diet**. Mom isn't around to make sure you eat your veggies, and "No," the four basic food groups for freshmen are not caffeine, fried foods, sugar and chocolate. It's common for freshmen to gain weight as they begin their college experience. Mid-night pizzas and beer are not calorie-free; it all adds up. Only you can control what you eat and how much is enough. On the other hand, some freshmen are so concerned about their weight that they become anorexic or bulimic. Neither one is pretty and both need counseling. Something is wrong when people starve their own bodies. If you don't know about Anorexia nervosa and Bulimia look them up. Get help or help someone else get help.

College Freshmen Ought to Know:

27.   that **Student Unions** are great places to meet friends and make friends. This may be an area on campus important to meet rides for commuting students. Visit the union often to find out what's happening on campus. Read the posters, talk to the people representing various groups or political or social issues. Enjoy yourself, play the games, watch TV and talk. But be careful not to spend too much time in the union having fun. Some of those students who seem to always be in the union are hiding from their academic studies and some of them won't be around next term!

College Freshmen Ought to Know:

28.   that you will be exposed to **new experiences** that aren't part of the academic schedule. You might be pressured to use drugs or purchase drugs. Drinking games and drinking to get drunk may be happening around you. Sexual experimenting may be part of your environment. Whatever the issue, drugs, alcohol or sex, only you as an individual can make a decision for yourself. You're on your own. Be prepared for how you will handle different situations. Don't be afraid of being seen as a loner. Don't feel you have to be seen as part of (or as a member of) a group. As soon as you take a position stating your opposition to what you don't want to do you will find others will

be happy to side with you. If you feel you could use some help or advice, don't be hesitant to ask resident hall assistants, directors, counselors, or advisors for their opinions. These people deal everyday with what you are now concerned about. It's new to you but not to them. It's much better to ask an employee of the college for some advice rather than a dorm-mate who is perhaps already involved in the problem. If someone keeps bothering you, get some advice on how to deal with them. You don't have to tolerate harassment of any type. We know freshmen experiment and make mistakes. You don't have to be alone in trying to solve a problem. Ask for help!

College Freshmen Ought to Know:

29. that **wearing a watch** is not uncool, it's critical. Being late can be embarrassing and you will quickly discover that no two clocks on campus ever show the same time, let alone the correct time.

College Freshmen Ought to Know:

30.   that you will be asked for either your **social security number** or your **student I.D. number** (given by the college) every time you do something official with the college. Memorize them. At some schools grades are posted by your student I.D. number; at other schools grades are posted by a code derived from part of your social security number. By the way, posting grades means taping a list of grades on a wall somewhere. (Know where and when this will happen.)

College Freshmen Ought to Know:

31. that **roommates** can become lasting friends or the entire evil empire. Living with someone requires a sensitivity perhaps never required on your part before. You will actually have to pay attention to when the other person wants to sleep with the lights out and the sound system off, what music you both can enjoy, how to be quiet when your roomie is sleeping, controlling your clothes and materials so they don't take over other people's territory, and all the other joys of living together. All roommates need to be sensitive to each other.

Keep talking to each other about problems that arise. Let people know what bothers you and expect to be told what bothers them, that's life. When continued clashes occur and you seem to be getting nowhere in resolving differences it's time to involve the resident dorm counselor. If differences can't be resolved request a room change. Sometimes this is possible, sometimes it's not and you're stuck until the next term.

College Freshmen Ought to Know:

32. that **dress** can be important. Most of the time college students dress casually and pay either a lot or little attention to style fads, depending on their mood. However, sometimes a particular dress code is necessary. If you are unsure, ask around to find out what would be appropriate. Remember the old saying, "You are what you eat"? Some would say it can also be "You are what you wear." Someone said that you never get a second chance to make a first impression, particularly whenever you go for an interview. Always dress

appropriately. When in doubt, dress up — not casual. Be neat and clean, with good manners. Men should be shaved or at least well trimmed. You might have a special costume that you identify as your interview outfit. Try to impress the interviewer with a serious, knowledgeable, organized, well groomed presence. Don't *ever* be late for an interview. Don't be flashy or too trendy. Don't wear anything that calls attention to itself — including jewelry and weird haircuts, unless you are auditioning for a rock band.

College Freshmen Ought to Know:

33. that sometimes you can **help yourself** to get into a more productive or creative mood by changing your environment for studying by simply dressing differently for the study session. Go to a different place on campus to do this particular chore or wear the best clothes you have to sit and write a particularly formal assignment. Some people have a particular hat or shoes that they say helps them with their tasks. Whatever works.

College Freshmen Ought to Know:

34. it's important to **keep track of your wallet** (money, credit cards, student I.D.) and keys at all times. You can be easily embarrassed and in trouble by not having your dorm or car key on the same side of the door that you find yourself. You must realize that money will disappear almost by itself, instantly. Never leave your purse, wallet, or change purse unlocked or unattended, even in your own dorm room.

College Freshmen Ought to Know:

35. that college **new student orientation** sessions should not be missed under 99% of circumstances. You not only get an opportunity to adjust to the feel of the campus and its students, but you learn about **campus services** and how they can help you succeed. Colleges are spending mega-bucks to provide student services including counseling, learning assistance, health, placement, etc. You are not getting your money's worth if you don't use them. One major difference between successful and unsuccessful students is that successful students learn where to find the people and services that can help them succeed. (Note: The Appendix lists some student services that may be available at your college. Review it, check off those that are available and where they are located.)

College Freshmen Ought to Know:

36. how to **write a check**. You'll need to know how to pay for books, telephone bills, credit card bills, etc. Bookstore managers tell me they must sometimes show people how to write out checks at the start of each new term. Get help with this as well as budgeting matters well before starting college.

Knowledge of Self

Items to help define the individual

College Freshmen Ought to Know:

37.   that you will need to **know yourself** in a way that perhaps you never realized. You are going to be expected to have not only thought about a lot of things but to have formed opinions about much of what was contemplated. These are going to be your thoughts, your feelings, your beliefs — not what your parents think, not what anybody else thinks or believes. This is you now, only you. Do you believe in God? (Be able to explain your response.) What do you really think about foreign students studying in this country? What do you really believe about Afro-Americans? About Whites? About Asian-Americans? What do you really believe about contemporary American

women? What are the top five priorities in your life right now? How sure are you? Why do you think you are sure? Are you registered to vote? (You had better be!) Are you sure you registered in the correct party?

The assumption is that if you are alive you must be thinking and you are attending college, a place where people think. You ought to know where you are at the beginning, look around yourself and try to understand who you are and why you got that way. In understanding yourself, it's important to keep an open mind. Perhaps things seem very clear now, but listen carefully and read well, you will find new ideas and your problem will be how to deal with them. Will you let these ideas change your life? This is what happens in college. It should happen. There are ideas and concepts in this world (and out of it also) that you know nothing about, absolutely nothing. And yet some of these will probably have profound effects on your life. Just know where you are now so that you can see where you want to go.

College Freshmen Ought to Know:

38. that, hopefully, you will have had **life experiences** that will have challenged your senses and beliefs and required you to think about your own position in life in relation to others, foods, clothes, customs, holy days, etc. Experiences are valuable when they give one a chance to view the world differently, to sense a sharing of environment with others and with nature. If you don't live in a large metropolitan city you ought to visit one for at least several days, eat food there, travel on its public transportation, look at its museums and

study the people who live there. You ought to stand on an isolated highway in corn country and look around three-hundred-sixty degrees. You see nothing but flat acres of corn as far as the eye can see. Think about the corn. Who planted it? Who will eat it? What makes it all work? You ought to dig for clams on a beach. Consider the sand. Where was it a thousand years ago? Where will it be a thousand years from now? Where will you be five years from now? What will you be doing?

College Freshmen Ought to Know:

39. the difference between **celebrity and hero**. Don't get confused. You ought to have some heros; people or characters that have qualities or attributes that you admire. Selecting heros reveals a lot about who you are, be aware of that. "One of the many distinctions between the celebrity and the hero... is that one lives only for self while the other acts to redeem society."[2] The hero has something of

[2] Betty Sue Flowers, ed., *Joseph Campbell The Power of Myth with Bill Moyers* (New York: Doubleday, 1988), p. xv.

value to offer others.   Also, a well informed member of an academic community will have some knowledge about leaders in various fields of human endeavor. You ought to be able to name and know something about:

an architect and one of his/her designs	a writer of novels
a composer	a well known doctor
a nationally known educator	a poet

Differences give one a chance to view the world differently.

Abilities

necessary for college success

College Freshmen Ought to Know:

40. that there are certain **intellectual abilities,** in addition to basic skills such as the ability to speak, write, and read in an articulate, educated manner, that are hoped for or assumed or even required as you begin any college level courses: the ability to locate countries around the globe, the ability to identify the major cities and topographic features of your country, the knowledge of biology — particularly how your own body functions, the ability to communicate in a

foreign language. Foreign language experience is critical to gain understanding of a culture other than your own, something necessary if you are to avoid thinking that your own country is the only country or always the best country. Other cultures can teach us much about life.[3]

[3] Suggestion from Dr. Jeffrey Victor, Professor, Sociology, Jamestown Community College, 1993.

College Freshmen Ought to Know:

41. that **good study skills** are vital to success. Better students already have good study skills. They were taught them or they learned them by trial and error. Whatever the case, good students have the ability to make great use of their **memory**. They can **read quickly** and **retain** the importance of what was read. They can **take good notes** that will help them study for exams. They know how to **predict test questions** and they know how to **study** for any particular kind of test. Good students will also plan ahead to build into their schedules all the hours necessary to get ready for an exam. They also know how not to worry themselves to death about exams. Regardless of one's academic standing, almost all students can benefit from even a brief study of a good **study skills textbook**. Locate one and practice its strategies.

College Freshmen Ought to Know:

42. that you must be able to **use a keyboard**. You must be able to type your own work, ideally using a computer. You cannot rely on others, even if you pay them. If you type your own work, you control every aspect, every detail; it's you. Plus, some professors are asking that written work be revised and re-submitted to qualify for a better grade. Quick editing and automated printing help this process. Know how or learn how to use a word processing program. It will make completing assignments easier. Besides, almost every kind of employment will require some time at a keyboard.

College Freshmen Ought to Know:

43. which **course materials to read** and how to read them. In some courses so much material is assigned that you cannot read it all so you must decide what to read and what to skip. Find out what is to be evaluated by paying attention in class (study the syllabus carefully), by asking previous students, by looking at old copies of exams, and specifically asking the instructor and/or the assistants. If you talk individually to the instructor and ask for more specific examples of material to be covered on the exam, be prepared to talk about examples of kinds of things that might be tested. The more you know when you ask the questions the more you will be able to decide what is going to be tested and what probably will not. The first response

you will get from a lot of instructors is that you must know all the material, have read everything; it's all equally important. But if you can ask questions about specific material you will be able to tell what is more important. Watch the instructor carefully to see where the emphasis is placed. In actually doing the reading, some material can be skimmed, some omitted, and some must be read and re-read. Don't ever read just to get through it. You are not concentrating on what you're doing. Also, put yourself in an environment that is quiet and uninterrupted; help yourself as much as possible. In most cases you must read the book — it will not be made into a movie.

College Freshmen Ought to Know:

44.   that a lot of discussion in college is based on **nominative distinction**. Being able to realize the differences between what is and what ought to be is important. Before you can wonder about what ought to be, you must know what is. The more you know about *everything* the better off you will be. What's the best way to learn about the most the fastest? Reading. Try playing a game in the library. Every time you are there, force yourself to check out a book

selected by following a formula you devise. Something like, say, randomly looking at a stack of books and removing the book that is on the second shelf from the bottom, seventh book from the right. Whatever it is, check it out, take it home, look it over. This is an interesting way to randomly introduce whole new areas to your life. However you do it, give yourself the advantage of knowing about everything; OK, as much as possible.

College Freshmen Ought to Know:

45.   that **education is not entertainment**. Sometimes education is fun and exciting, but a lot of the time it is not. It's just plain hard work. Lectures can be boring. There will be no exciting visual image change every two seconds as on MTV. Keep busy taking good notes. For some lecturers English is a second language and you must pay very close attention just to understand the language let alone the concepts. Some faculty have huge egos with elitist behaviors that don't allow easy contact with lowly students. Elitist attitudes shouldn't be in education, but they are, and you will have to get through some of them to achieve your goal. That's life. If college degrees were easy to earn, everyone would have one. One of the first things a college degree says about you is that you can survive.

College Freshmen Ought to Know:

46. that you can **practice taking good notes** by making a game out of taking notes while watching a news broadcast. Take notes for ten minutes, then compare them with others and see who has the **most important details**. Learning what is relevant is important. Perhaps the color tie the reporter was wearing is utterly useless information and you missed the point of the story. You are not a recording machine and all that is said need not be written; learning to select what is important is crucial to your success. Professors who write on the board, for example, are not just exercising their wrists. If they write, you write. It's probably important.

College Freshmen Ought to Know:

47. about some basic **computer programs**. You need not know how to operate all the programs, but you ought to be familiar with one basic program in word processing. Once you understand one program it's not that difficult to learn another. Regardless of your major, be familiar with as many of the following computer terms as possible: *Word, Word Perfect, Write Now, Lotus, Spell Check*, spread sheet, access, backup copy, *BASIC*, binary, bit, *CAD/CAM*, chip, *COBOL*, crt, data, disk, floppy disk, fiber optics, *FORTRAN*, hard copy, hardware, integer, K, log on/off, microfiche, modem, mouse, *PASCAL*, program, Qwerty keyboard, *RAM*, real time, *ROM*, search, task, terminal.

College Freshmen Ought to Know:

48. that **various kinds of tests** will be given in different courses. Make sure you check with your professors about the kinds of tests they plan to give: objective vs. essay, unit tests vs. a comprehensive final (an exam that will cover all material assigned from the beginning of the course through the last class meeting), etc. Ask other students who have had a particular professor about the class and tests. How should you take notes, read, and study? Study skills books can also help. Tips like responding exactly to directions like "describe," "compare and contrast," "list," etc., can improve your success. Question early, plan early, and work toward your plan. You'll be better prepared for all kinds of tests.

College Freshmen Ought to Know:

49. that **oral exams** are not cute little chats with the instructor. An oral exam is a thorough shakedown of the student which will usually reveal to the instructor much more than the student thinks is being communicated. Between the content and the delivery, the experience can disclose great preparation or not much of anything. Usually the student will be given an immediate grade. Advanced preparation and being quizzed by a fellow classmate will help you prepare for oral exams.

College Freshmen Ought to Know:

50. their **campus**. Get a campus map and orient yourself. Where will you be living? Which way is north? Some professors will offer bonus points on exams (having nothing to do with geography) that will ask the student to list each state and/or geographic landmark contiguous to the state the college is in. But it's just good sense to know the entire campus. Where can you park your car? How long does it take to walk from one place to another? Some instructors will make reference to something on the south side of the lecture room building. Know in which direction that would be. Find out where campus services can be found. You may have a need and little time to search. Start from the first day, explore!

College Freshmen Ought to Know:

51. that many students getting ready for college now are in a very dangerous situation and do not realize it. Many students have come through schooling that has not given them the **academic preparation** they need to succeed in college. Their high school grades may have been good grades, and yet they will not be able to operate in the basic skills areas at a high enough level to succeed. This is where counseling, the learning assistance center, and other services can come

College Freshmen Ought to Know:

in real handy. They can help you set realistic goals through placement test scores and assist with guidance on careers. Advisement centers can also suggest remedial courses to improve your abilities so you're able to compete successfully in more difficult courses. Remember, in college as in life, if you realize a weakness exists, get help. If you do, you'll survive and your degree will hold the same value as everyone else's.

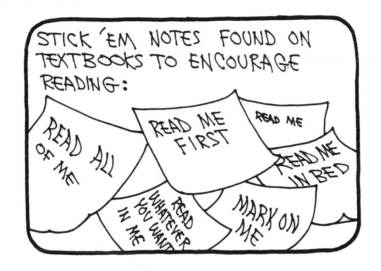

Readings

**to develop background and understandings
for successful students**

College Freshmen Ought to Know:

52. that almost all of a **college education will be based on reading**. There is an enormous assumption on the part of the college that you have been participating in reading as you have prepared yourself for college. It is through reading that you will have shared experiences with others and learned about the world. The more you have read and thought about what you have read the better off you will be.

In order for students to have some similarities of experiences to more fully participate in college, **reading lists** are created. Many colleges create their own list and hope that students will have read most, a lot,

College Freshmen Ought to Know:

some, or several titles from the list. Of course, the better students will have read more, and that's a great reason why they will continue to be better students. Even if you haven't read a lot of worthy titles, at the very least, you must be familiar with the existence of some of the best works written. To understand reading lists you should look at a copy of: *Reading Lists for College-Bound Students*, 2nd. edition, ARCO, 1993.[4] This book has specific reading lists from over 100 colleges. It also has a list of the 100 most recommended titles. This list is annotated. You ought to read carefully each entry and become familiar

[4] Doug Estell, Michele L. Satchwell, and Patricia S. Wright, *Reading Lists for College-Bound Students*, 2nd ed. (New York: ARCO, Prentice Hall, 1993).

with the author's name and the title. The ones you have read will appear as old friends and, hopefully, some of the entries will become intriguing enough to get you to read them. What follows is a very abbreviated list from the list of 100. How many of these have you read? How many of these have your fellow students read?

Novels and Short Stories
Bellow, Saul, *Seize the Day*
Bronte, Emily, *Wuthering Heights*
Camus, Albert, *The Stranger*
Cervantes, Miguel de, *Don Quixote*
Conrad, Joseph, *Heart of Darkness*
Defoe, Daniel, *Robinson Crusoe*
Ellison, Ralph, *Invisible Man*

Faulkner, William, *The Sound and the Fury*
Fitzgerald, F. Scott, *The Great Gatsby*
Hawthorne, Nathaniel, *The Scarlet Letter*
James, Henry, *The Turn of the Screw*
Kafka, Franz, *The Trial*
Malamud, Bernard, *The Assistant*
Morrison, Toni, *Sula*
Olsen, Tillie, *Tell Me a Riddle*
Paton, Alan, *Cry, the Beloved Country*
Poe, Edgar Allan, *Great Tales and Poems*
Salinger, J.D., *The Catcher in the Rye*
Swift, Jonathan, *Gulliver's Travels*
Twain, Mark, *The Adventures of Huckleberry Finn*
Updike, John, *Rabbit Run*
Welty, Eudora, *Thirteen Stories*

Drama

Miller, Arthur, *Death of a Salesman*
Shakespeare, William, *Hamlet*
Shaw, George Bernard, *Pygmalion*
Sophocles, *Oedipus Rex*
Wilder, Thornton, *Our Town*

Miscellaneous

Bible
Darwin, Charles, *Origin of Species*
Hamilton, Edith, *Mythology*
Machiavelli, Niccolo, *The Prince*
Plato, *Republic*
Thoreau, Henry David, *Walden*

Poetry

Look over this anthology and select a few poems about which you would be able to write something: Allison, Alexander, Ed., *Norton Anthology of Poetry*.

College Freshmen Ought to Know:

53. to have a list of your **own favorite titles** (from the above mentioned lists, or not). Be able to write about the central ideas and characters in your list. Know the themes and then consider what their appeal may reveal about yourself. Now there's a subject for a writing assignment!

54. the **book is *always* (usually, often) better** than the movie!

55. it's **never too late** to start reading. It will open whole new worlds, universes, and galaxies to you. When you read you're never lonely.

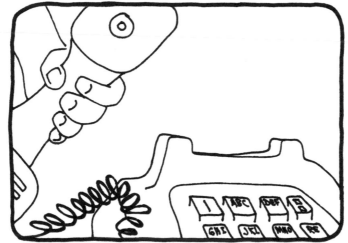

Mom! The big deal says he's Matriculated - is that good or bad?

Definitions and Customs

in college life

College Freshmen Ought to Know:

56. that the **degree** is what it's all about. Normally, 60 credit hours will be required for an Associate's degree; 120 credit hours for a Bachelor's degree; 30 graduate credit hours for a Master's degree, and 90 graduate credit hours for the Doctor of Philosophy degree. Master's degrees and Doctor of Philosophy degrees are awarded only by graduate schools and admission to graduate schools requires the Bachelor's degree.

There are approximately 29 varieties of Associate degrees; 285 varieties of Bachelor's degrees; 120 varieties of Master of Arts degrees; 270 varieties of Master of Science degrees; 61 varieties of Doctor's degrees.[5]   The Doctor's degree is the most advanced degree and is conferred for professional, research, or honorary achievement. In some fields the Master's degree is considered the terminal, or highest level of degree achieved. The most awarded degrees are:

A.A.	Associate in Arts	A.A.S.	Associate in Applied Science
A.S.	Associate in Science	B.A.	Bachelor in Arts
B.S.	Bachelor in Science	M.A.	Master of Arts
M.S.	Master of Science	Ph. D.	Doctor of Philosophy

[5] David A. Lockmiller, "Degrees, Academic," *The Encyclopedia Of Education*, 1971 ed., III, 25.

College Freshmen Ought to Know:

57. that traditionally the terms: **university, college, school, division, and department** are here listed in hierarchical order of decreasing diversity, completeness, and speciality of academic curriculum offerings. **University** is an umbrella term used to include all of its colleges, schools, divisions, and departments associated under a united administrative structure. **College** is an independent self-governing unit for the study of particular disciplines. Colleges can operate separately or can be included within a university. Many institutions calling themselves colleges operate more like universities and the terms can begin to lose distinction. A university usually has sev-

eral colleges, perhaps a **school** or two, and then within the colleges and/or schools one may find **divisions**, and finally the smallest unit of collegial organization, the **department**.

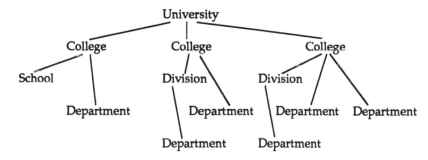

College Freshmen Ought to Know:

58. that **Liberal Arts and Sciences** generally refers to a curriculum of study in the natural sciences, social sciences, and the humanities.

59. that **Natural Sciences** generally refer to the study of "natural objects, including biology, geology, mineralogy, physics, and chemistry."[6]

[6] Webster's Student Dictionary, G. & C. Merriam Co., p. 541

College Freshmen Ought to Know:

60. that **Humanities** generally refers to the disciplines: architecture, art, dance, drama, English, foreign language, history, literature, music, philosophy, theology, jurisprudence, and archaeology.

National Endowment for the Humanities (1965) definition: "language, both modern and classic; linguistics; literature; history; jurisprudence; philosophy; archaeology; the history, criticism, theory and practice of the arts; and those aspects of the social sciences which have humanistic content and employ humanistic methods."[7]

[7] Bruce McPherson, "Humanities, Education in the," *Academic American Encyclopedia*, 1988 ed., H, 300.

College Freshmen Ought to Know:

61. that **Social Sciences** generally refers to study in anthropology, economics, history, political science, social psychology, sociology, criminology, and law. Other disciplines sometimes included are education, geography, psychiatry, statistics, and religion.[8]

---

[8] Charles M. Bonjean, "Social Science," *The World Book Encyclopedia*, 1990 ed. Richard E. Gross, "Social Science," *Encyclopedia Americana*, 1988 ed.

College Freshmen Ought to Know:

62. that **discipline or field** can refer to sports training and location but in the academic world these terms refer to specialized areas of study such as cultural anthropology, comparative religion, forensic chemistry, etc.

College Freshmen Ought to Know:

63.   that some students will be working toward a **Certificate**, not a degree. Certificates require less hours and courses than a degree and are usually limited to a very specialized area of academic activity. Some certificates can be earned without any other college experience while others can require that the student have a Bachelor's degree before even enrolling in the program.

College Freshmen Ought to Know:

64.   that a **two-year degree** may take 3 years and a **four-year degree** may take 5 years to complete. In some schools almost half of the graduates are taking longer to finish the requirements for degrees than used to be the case. Many reasons exist for the longer time necessary to finish the work: student working schedules, caring for children or parents, changing a major and thus taking some courses that will not count toward those required by the new major, not taking a full load each term, loss of credits due to transferring, required to take a course or two for remedial study that will not count toward the degree, etc.

College Freshmen Ought to Know:

65. the **total cost** of attending a particular college or university for all the terms necessary to earn a degree. What will be the starting salary in your occupational area with your degree/background/experience? If you are entering an occupation like public education, social work, or health care, the prestige of a high tuition college may not make a difference in your salary.   If you have student loans, how will

you repay large tuition debt with a small salary? If money is no problem or you simply want the experience that some more costly colleges offer, then, of course, go wherever you feel most comfortable. Just be very careful to get the most out of your educational dollars in considering which college to attend.

College Freshmen Ought to Know:

66. that the cost of **tuition** covers only about a third of the cost of keeping the college in operation. The other two-thirds revenue necessary comes from various sources largely depending on whether or not the college is private or public; public colleges rely on tax dollars, federal, state, and local with private colleges encouraging philanthropy as much as possible. All college presidents will tell you that they spend great amounts of their time and energy fund raising for their schools. This is why schools having large **endowments** can put inter-

est earned from the endowments toward operating expenses and are at a great advantage. **Operating expenses** are the day-to-day costs of the operation of the college: salaries, utilities, maintenance, supplies, etc. **Capital expenses** are those incurred for building projects; named buildings usually indicate a donation of money from that person or estate toward the cost of building the structure. Notice that you will probably never see a **memorial** sewer system on a campus.

College Freshmen Ought to Know:

67. that the **length of college terms** vary. The most frequently used teaching schedule is the **semester**, which is approximately 15 weeks long. Two semesters comprise an academic year. Some schools are on the **quarter** system, which has three 10 or 11-week schedules for the academic year with an additional quarter offered in the summer. Other schools offer the **trimester,** which has three terms sched-

uled throughout the year. Usually a student will enroll in two of the three to gain an academic year. Be sure to understand the teaching schedule when you enroll. Final exams may be included during the regular schedule of classes, but sometimes finals are offered with their own schedule after the teaching schedule is completed. Do not miss a final exam!

College Freshmen Ought to Know:

68.   that the **Financial Aid** office will have wanted you to fill out all the **necessary forms** a long, long time ago. There are several important forms to prepare if you, as most students, are going to request financial grants, loans, or any aid other than from family. Once you figure out the cost of tuition, room and board, books, and all the other expenses associated with a full year at college, you need to devise a plan to gather the funds. Years before attending your first year of college is not too early to plan how to pay for it all. Early planning

school grades and the almost necessity of obtaining grants to offset the high costs. Get current rules and regulations from the Financial Aid office. If you qualify as *financially independent* from your family, determine how this will benefit you. What other kinds of help can you get from relatives, friends, or community organizations? The **Bursar's office** (Business office) is where you will end up paying the fees charged, so know where both it and the **Financial Aid office** are located on campus.

College Freshmen Ought to Know:

69.   that **admission** to the college is necessary in order to be permitted to register for courses. One must apply for admission to the college at the Admissions office. It is important to meet deadlines for applications to colleges. Some colleges require application for admission ten months before the beginning of the term — others require application only days before the term begins. Also note that some degree programs require special admission apart from the actual admission into the institution, (i.e., some accounting programs). Be sure to know what is required by both the institution and the field of study to which you are applying. Know the deadlines!

College Freshmen Ought to Know:

70. that **matriculation** happens when the Admissions office has accepted your application to begin work toward a particular stated degree. In many cases the Admissions office is only the informer of the news, and the actual decisions of acceptance or rejection are made by a committee of the department, school, or college to which you applied. **Why care about your matriculation date?** Because your matriculation date determines the current catalog with its rules and regulations in effect for your degree requirements. Keep your first copy in a safe place. You may need it someday.

College Freshmen Ought to Know:

71.   that **registration** is the process of officially enrolling in courses. This is done by the Registrar's office and can involve standing in long lines. At some institutions, computer registration is handled by registration personnel using computer terminals. At a lot of schools one can register for classes by mail. If this is possible, do it. It might save hours of standing in lines in front of registration tables. The registration process begins months before the start of classes. The longer you wait to register the more chance you have of a particular class being closed, or filled, by the time you try to enroll. Some classes fill up so fast it seems as though they are filled before anyone can begin to register.

College Freshmen Ought to Know:

72. that **catalogs** not only are important to give you information about the college and its programs, policies, and regulations, but the catalog in effect at the time of your first enrollment at that college is a **contract** between you and the college. If you follow the instructions in the catalog for a particular degree you shall be awarded that degree. For example, the college cannot require you to take new courses or require a higher grade point average once you have started your course work for a degree.

College Freshmen Ought to Know:

73.   that **major** and **minor** and **distribution** requirements refer to numbers of course credit hours applied in various categories which will total the required hours for the degree. Read the college catalog to determine which courses are necessary to fulfill requirements for your major/minor. Distribution requirements refer to courses required from various parts of the college curriculum. Something like a Chinese menu, one from column A, one from column B, etc. The attempt is to insure that graduates have experience in particular academic areas in which they might not normally enroll. Something like vitamins, they're good for you!

College Freshmen Ought to Know:

74. that traditionally, **course numbering** would indicate the level of the course offered: 100's freshmen level, 200's sophomore level, 300's junior level, 400's senior level, 500's graduate level. Remedial couses are often quite valuable in helping you complete your degree but offer no credit. They are usually numbered below 100, (i.e., 098, 096, etc.).

College Freshmen Ought to Know:

75.   that your **advisor** actually can be helpful. Most students are assigned a faculty advisor in the field in which they are majoring. When meeting with your advisor you must have some preliminary information. What are your goals? What do you want to be doing five years from now? If transferring, do you have a catalog from the transfer school to help you decide what to take *before* you transfer? These kinds of questions will be asked by your advisor. If you don't have clear goals, you are not alone. Tell your advisor. He/she is there to guide you toward some clear goals and good decisions. Maybe you can arrange to select some introductory courses in a variety of fields. An internship may be possible in a career field that interests you. A visit to the Career Planning office might help you investigate career options. These are all suggestions your advisor can give you. Ulti-

mately however, these decisions must be made by you. An advisor can only help you help yourself.

Every once in a while an advisor does not give the time or interest to do the best job of advising. If you are in this situation, politely try to get a different advisor. The Advisement Center or your department chairperson can usually help you switch advisors. Sometimes, however, your options may be limited. Your advisor may be the only faculty member in this particular field, etc. You must know the catalog, the schedules, the rules, and watch out for yourself because you are on your own! Try to gather additional advice from upper classmen and other faculty members.

College Freshmen Ought to Know:

76.   that to be considered a **full-time student** you must be enrolled in at least **12 semester credit hours** for the term. This is important if you need to be full-time for financial aid qualifications. If you are receiving financial aid as a full-time student, be careful not to drop (withdraw from) a course during the term that would then lower your status to a part-time student. The rules are always changing but I know of students who had to refund part of their financial aid because they became part-time. Also, some students had the money deducted from what they were eligible for the following term. Either way it's a financial jolt to students. Be careful, it may cost you!

College Freshmen Ought to Know:

77. that when filling out a **class schedule** the student must be careful to avoid time conflicts — two classes that overlap in time. Also, try to avoid enrolling in a class at one end of the campus with only the usual ten minutes to move to the opposite end of the campus for the next class. Alas, sometimes this cannot be avoided — consider roller blades? Invariably the first class instructor will always keep the class past the time limit giving even fewer minutes to cross campus for the next class. Also, note carefully the meeting times for classes. Some will begin and end at odd times and most will meet two or three times a week, although in summer sessions there might be meetings six days a week, a real killer when much reading is required.

College Freshmen Ought to Know:

78. a **pre-requisite** means there is at least one other course you must take (and pass) before you can enroll in this course. The pre-requisite course will be listed so that you can easily determine if you qualify for enrollment or not. **Co-requisite** means that when you enroll in this particular course you must also, same term, be enrolled in the one listed as the co-requisite course.

College Freshmen Ought to Know:

79. that normally, each **credit hour** is a unit of measurement in college. Each credit course is assigned a particular number of credit hours, depending on the number of times the class meets and the number of clock hours it meets during the semester, or quarter, or trimester. Three is the most common number of credits for a semester course.

College Freshmen Ought to Know:

80.   that **imputed courses** are taken with no credit applied toward graduation. They are usually remedial courses required to raise the skill level of the student in reading, writing, or math. They can be some of the most worthwhile courses you take in college.

College Freshmen Ought to Know:

81. that some courses, notably **freshmen introductory courses**, will be very large (several hundred students) sitting in something like a small auditorium with the professor on stage wearing a microphone. TV cameras may also be used to show close-up shots of whatever the professor is trying to illustrate. You will hardly have a chance to ask questions in such a setting, be prepared to ask/discuss at the next meeting of small "discussion" or "study" sessions that you have for this course. The large lecture meetings might be held once a week with several meetings of the smaller groups each week. The small group meetings are usually run by graduate students. Don't miss these; it's easier to ask questions and get help.

College Freshmen Ought to Know:

82. that **Drop and Add** is that brief time at the beginning of the term when students can drop courses in which they are currently enrolled and may also add a course that they would now like to pick up. Be careful when dropping courses that you are not just trying to avoid difficult material. If it's a required course for you, consider getting tutorial help and assistance from academic study skill centers on campus. You will need to take the course sometime. If you take it later what will you do to be more successful? Get some help from tutors or assistants. Most of us need help in some academic area. We're not all brilliant in every discipline . . . look at Einstein!

College Freshmen Ought to Know:

83. that there are things called **overload cards**, or some similar name, that if signed by the instructor of the course in which you are trying to enroll will permit the Registrar's office to enroll your name in a filled or **closed** course. Sometimes you might convince an instructor to sign an overload card for you if you have a compelling enough reason. That your best friend is already in the class is not a compelling reason. Faculty members also realize that there are always a few students who drop the course without ever showing up at the class. You might remind the instructor of this.

College Freshmen Ought to Know:

84.   that one must **Withdraw** from a course not wanted. If you want to drop out of a course for any reason you must do it officially by completing the proper forms available at the Registrar's office. If you simply stop attending the course and forget about it, you will receive a grade anyway. And that grade will undoubtedly be an F.

College Freshmen Ought to Know:

85. how to calculate your **Grade Point Average**, or **GPA**.
Sample: (Based on a semester or quarter term)

4.0 scale		Final Grade	Points
A=4	course 1	3 credit hours X B (3) =	9
B=3	course 2	3 credit hours X C (2) =	6
C=2	course 3	4 credit hours X B (3) =	12
D=1	course 4	2 credit hours X A (4) =	8
F=0			
		12 credit hours	35

35 points divided by 12 credit hours = 2.92   **GPA = 2.92**

Your GPA counts from your first term! It builds upon itself and is hard to improve if it becomes low. Think about that from the beginning! (Investigate the formula specific to your college's term length.)

College Freshmen Ought to Know:

86. that the college actually is interested in having you succeed. **Retention** (keeping) of students is vital for many reasons. Some of the most important: colleges are evaluated by what they produce; faculty get retrenched (released from contract) without students; more students translates into more tuition and more financial aid dollars to work with. Without upper classmen to teach, faculty can get bored teaching only introductory courses. Larger issue: what's going to happen to failed students? What will they be doing in our society? Will those who succeed in college end up supporting those who don't?

College Freshmen Ought to Know:

87. that **academic probation** is a period, usually one term, in which the student is given a chance to improve his/her over-all grade point average. At the end of the probationary term if the grade point average does not meet or exceed the stated requirement the student will normally be dismissed from the college, called **academic dismissal**. Also, the college catalog will list the required grade point average and credit hours necessary to remain in good academic standing. First term freshmen sometimes have slightly lower requirements. Warnings are sometimes used instead of probation for first term freshmen.

College Freshmen Ought to Know:

88.   that a **syllabus** is a collection of information about the course. It usually contains the following: course description, goals and objectives of the course, reading assignments and due dates, an outline of the course that usually includes course requirements including what will be evaluated and how the evaluation will take place. This is the key to the course. If you do not receive one of these the first day of course — watch out. You may be in a class in which the instructor will change the rules as you go along or the instructor may be only a

day ahead of you in the preparations and readings for the course. Read the syllabus carefully about attendance policy, due dates for papers, and exam dates. Hopefully you will have several tests and/or a variety of times to be evaluated. Pity the unfortunate student who will have only a final exam, no papers, no quizzes, nothing else to have measured failure or success during the entire term. Everything rests on that last day. This is questionable educational methodology, but you will still find faculty performing this way.

College Freshmen Ought to Know:

89.   that a **curve** grading scale is based on the highest score attained in the class. The instructor will take the highest score and determine all grades by subtracting a percent (perhaps 10%), from that starting point, a percent for A's, the B's, the C's, the D's, and the failure point. The **standard** grading scale or straight grading scale is usually 90 or 93 to 100 an A, 80 or 86 to 89 or 92 is a B, and so on. In using the straight scale it makes no difference what the students score on the exam. The grades are distributed into the scale without influencing one another. There may be no A grades. Students would prefer using curve grading and some instructors do use it, but others will use the straight scale.

Example of Standard Grade Scale	Example of Curve Grade Scale
90-100 A	83-100 A (83 highest grade in class)
80-89 B	73-82 B
70-79 C	63-72 C
60-69 D	53-62 D
0 -59 F	0 -52 F

College Freshmen Ought to Know:

90.   an **Audit** grade carries **no** academic credit. It's given for attendance in a course that may not apply to your degree but would prove valuable for some special interest, (i.e., travel abroad, career, etc.). An Audit grade can be received if the student registers for one. All the regular fees must be paid and through discussion and permission with the instructor the student is permitted to sit in on the class and participate as fully as discussed with the instructor. Audit grade students may or may not take exams. Students who audit a course are doing so only for the experience they can gain, not for any hours added to their college record.

College Freshmen Ought to Know:

91.   that a student must request an **Incomplete** grade for a course. An instructor will not usually offer one; it's up to the student to ask. Incomplete grades are usually given *only* for substantial reasons, as in an accident that kept you in the hospital for four weeks causing you to miss many classes. And you must be able to prove it! Incomplete grades are never given simply because you need more time. So does everyone else. If you receive an Incomplete final grade, notice the deadline for performing the required work. If the exams and/or papers, etc. are not submitted by the deadline, the Incomplete grade will automatically change to an F. In most institutions the maximum time to work on an Incomplete grade is one calendar year, but some instructors will offer as little time as two weeks. Once you receive an Incomplete grade do not forget about it.

College Freshmen Ought to Know:

92. that **Pass/Fail** or **Credit/No Credit** is a grade option that permits a student to register for a course on a different grading system than the usual A, B, C, D, or F scale. The student will receive a **Pass** or **Credit** grade if all work was satisfactory and if not satisfactory the grade would be **Fail** or **No Credit**. If the grade is **Pass** or **Credit** those hours will be added toward the degree. Students might select this option for a course they wished to take but were concerned about getting less than an A grade that would hurt their grade point aver-

age. Students competing for medical school, for example, might be concerned about taking an art studio course and receiving a B grade instead of an A. Caution should be used in selecting this option since many transfer schools do not like to see this Pass/Fail grade. They want to see an actual grade. Also, there is usually a limit on the number of hours one can take under this option and apply toward a degree. The limit is usually 12 to 16 credit hours.

College Freshmen Ought to Know:

93.   that courses designated as **lecture** will be taught by the lecture method, a body talking to a large group of students. **Seminars** are small gatherings of perhaps two to a dozen students. **Workshops** are usually offered to address one specific topic and usually last only a few sessions. All styles of teaching formats may or may not carry academic credit.

College Freshmen Ought to Know:

94.   that a **lab course** is one in which a laboratory meeting time and location is in addition to the lecture portion of the course. In most cases a student must register for both the **lecture** and the **lab** sections for the course. These may not necessarily be taught by the same instructor and may not even be taught in the same building.

College Freshmen Ought to Know:

95.   that a **studio course** is offered by some art, music, theater, and drama departments and is structured for students to actually work on course assignments during the class meeting time. It is not a lecture course. Usually, the studio class will meet in actual hours twice the number of credit hours per week. (3 credit hour studio course meets 6 clock hours per week; if in a professional art school 6 clock hours per week will equal 6 credit hours for the course.)

College Freshmen Ought to Know:

96. that **recording lectures** requires permission from the instructor. Usually instructors are pleased to have a student record the lecture, but ask permission. Learning disabled students may find this especially valuable. However, understand that recording lectures can be difficult and give a false sense of security. The recorder may not pick up all the words. Also, just because it's all recorded does not mean it will play back in a more orderly, condensed, precise outline form of information as in well taken notes. It will also not play back the visual materials presented. If you did take good notes, the playback might help to augment the notes. Remember that an hour of recorded lecture will take another hour to hear again. Do you really have the time?

College Freshmen Ought to Know:

97. what **plagiarism** is. Plagiarism is claiming as one's own the creative efforts of someone else. The material stolen may be written, verbal, visual, or auditory. Some high school students get in the habit of simply copying work from anywhere and applying it to wherever they wish with no thought that the original is "owned" by someone. Indeed, it is most likely protected by copyright. Don't assume you can lift just a few phrases or sentences here and there and no one will

notice. Faculty are excellent at recognizing such misuse. All of a sudden the student paper shifts to one of authority speaking! Of course it stands out. Also, most faculty are familiar with almost everything published in their field — assume they know it well. Create your own work. Just give yourself the time it's going to require. The penalties for plagiarism are meant to be harsh, typically failure of the project or failure of the course or even expulsion from the college.

College Freshmen Ought to Know:

98.   that **networking** is not a term referring to those who fix nets for tuna fishing. It is a dynamic for communicating and is often the only way you will learn about some things. **Networking** is the process of making connections with other people because of a particular common link. That link might be professional, social, from a very temporary or casual contact, or from a group that you will be associated with for years. Whatever the reason for the original contact, keep in touch with these people. Often these contacts are the only way you will find out about opportunities for yourself, like grants or jobs.

College Freshmen Ought to Know:

99.   the **campus book store**, whatever it may be called, will collect a lot of your money. Students will gripe about the prices of new and used textbooks and sometimes used book prices will be quite close to the new book price (interesting choice to be made there).

At some colleges you must take the text to class the first day — it will be used. Therefore you'll have to actually find out what books will be required for each course and instructor. You must at least know the titles. Asking for the blue and red one won't work.

At other colleges, do not buy textbooks until you have attended your first class in order to find out which books are going to be used by that instructor. Save your textbook purchase receipts in case you need to exchange the text. If instructors are switched you may need a different text. Bookstores usually have good information on which texts go with which instructors; also for any other required materials for courses.

College Freshmen Ought to Know:

100. that it's OK to purchase **used textbooks**. Look the books over carefully but they are usually examined closely by either the publisher's representatives or the bookstore and found to contain all the pages and not be too badly marked for resale. Be careful if you are buying books from off-campus bookstores or from other students. If you buy the wrong book by mistake you might not be able to exchange it, let alone get a refund.

College Freshmen Ought to Know:

101. that at the end of the term you will get offers from the bookstore to **buy back your textbooks**. Sometimes you must decide at the beginning of a term whether you will be doing this. Good learning often means marking and actively using your text. In the long haul, you'll need to decide whether the money you'll receive for your book will outweigh the benefit of really using it for your education. Therefore, decide carefully which books to sell and which to keep. However, aside from that, books that will never be used for reference in

your personal library might be good to sell. But those that might be of use for future papers or general reference should be kept. Expensive books that will never go out of date, like art history texts, ought to be saved. Compared to the cost paid, the buy-back rate is sometimes so low it makes more sense to keep the book.

Note: Don't sell this book. It has a good index so keep it handy. You'll find lots of occasions to use it as you advance through college.

College Freshmen Ought to Know:

102. where the **library** is and how to use it. A lot of time will be spent here. Know what facilities are available to assist you (i.e., computer terminals, microfiche, library loan arrangements, etc.). Pay close attention and write down instructions when being shown how to use the various systems. Also, find a quiet place somewhere in the library where you can go to really get serious studying done. A very quiet and secluded place is needed. Go regularly and you'll be surprised how much you can accomplish.

College Freshmen Ought to Know:

103. that **libraries are changing fast**. The days of the card catalog are nearly over. Today, libraries are the centers of communications with emphasis on individual terminals for students to be able to link-up global networks for instant communication regarding anything, but particularly the existence, location, and availability of research materials. Much work will be done right from the screen itself and from printouts requested. **Reserve readings** are materials: books, articles, clippings, photographs, etc. that the instructor has arranged for the library to release for student use for only a specific period of time. If the instructor announces availability of reserve material, ask at the circulation desk for the information for your class. Don't wait. Others may be using it when you most need it. Plan ahead.

College Freshmen Ought to Know:

104. that **distance learning**, using satellite video, is changing the way many courses will be taught. One professor in front of a video camera lectures/demonstrates to students spread over wide geographic areas. Students viewing TV monitors with an up-link are able to ask questions and have dialog with the professor. This is an example of **interactive** education.

College Freshmen Ought to Know:

105. that a **transcript** is the official record of your academic history at an institution. It will have listed by dates all course work, final grades, and any academic honors or academic warnings, probations, or dismissals. An official transcript will have an embossed seal of the college on it. This is the proof that not only have you attended these courses, you have earned these grades. You will most likely be requested to submit a copy of your transcript along with every serious job application you make.

College Freshmen Ought to Know:

106. that your **resume** is a distant chore waiting to be filled out, but it gets filled with only things that are going to make you look good. It helps to be able to plan some of those good-looking items. When you begin applying for real jobs your resume is the device that shows how serious you are and what a good addition you would be to the inter-viewing organization. Besides good grades and references from fac-ulty members who actually know you, try to have experiences in the resume that help you stand out from the rest of the crowd. Intern-ships and tutoring are excellent items to be able to list. **Internships** will give you actual experience in the field enabling you to learn more

about what actually happens. For example, two college interns helped in the development and publication of this very text. Also, **tutoring** jobs are not only the best way to earn money and keep on top of your field but listing your duties on your resume should prove helpful whether you're applying to graduate school or a job in business or industry.

(Note: Remember to ask internship and/or tutoring supervisors for a letter of reference. They can be a good addition to your resume.)

College Freshmen Ought to Know:

107. that a **transfer** student is one who has earned college credit hours at one institution and is now transferring those hours to a new institution in order to help meet final requirements for a degree. Students transfer for a number of different reasons. Colleges accommodate such students by making special arrangements among themselves to accept transferring credits under most circumstances. However, most colleges will only transfer courses with grades of C or higher. Also, there will be a limit on the number of hours permitted to transfer.

If you are planning to transfer from one institution to another, you should investigate the process. Research the requirements of the new college to be sure credits will transfer. Speak with your advisor about your plans. Some may assist by making a call to the department at the new institution to clarify your understandings. Begin the process of investigation early.

PURCHASING TEXTBOOKS:

" I'll TAKE ONE GREEN ONE, NOT TOO THICK, ONE WITH LOTS OF PICTURES, AND THE ONE WITH THE YELLOW STRIP. OH YES, THAT CUTE LITTLE ONE ON THE LOWER SHELF... "

Sometimes it makes sense to audit.

College Freshmen Ought to Know:

that the following items (108-117) deal with the definitions and customs particular to post-graduation, faculty, and the institution. Understand them, you won't be a freshman forever and it may help your long term goal setting.

108. that **graduate work** has to do with activity beyond or after attaining a Bachelor's degree. A **graduate student** has already earned the Bachelor's degree. **Post graduate** study refers to courses taken after a student already has earned the Bachelor's degree. **Post Doctoral** study would be for those already holding the Doctor of Philosophy degree. If you're planning for any of these, start now. It might seem out of place, but so did your parents' discussion of college in 6th grade. What impact did that have?

College Freshmen Ought to Know:

109. that **academic rank** is what it's all about for faculty members. Usually, the lowest rank for a full-time faculty position is Instructor, with promotion to **Assistant Professor**, **Associate Professor**, and finally to **Professor**. Promotion is far from just time served at an institution, although that is also considered — usually at least four or five years at each level. Original research, contributions to the community, and in some cases the ability to walk on water are all considered by the committee for promotion. Many faculty would like nothing better than to spend time with students. However, this is not high school. Realize they need to balance their priorities as well.

College Freshmen Ought to Know:

110. that **tenure** is achieved by a faculty member after successfully serving the required probationary period, usually five years. The idea is that if the individual faculty member is a poor teacher, evidence to support non-renewal of the contract can be gathered in the first several years. Once tenure is granted it is much more difficult to remove a faculty member from the school. Normally, only a substantiated charge of immoral behavior or a drop of student enrollment are rea-

sons for revoking tenure to a faculty member. Part-time faculty never have tenure. **Academic freedom** is the prime reason for having this status. It protects faculty job security from arbitrary and threatening actions for supporting unpopular, novel, unusual, or misunderstood positions within their academic discipline. Faculty have the obligation and must have the freedom to tell it like it is.

College Freshmen Ought to Know:

111. that **sabbatical leave** is sometimes granted to full-time faculty members to continue their original research/production away from the campus. Sabbatical leaves are granted annually to a small percentage of the faculty. The leaves are usually for one full term with continued full salary, or an entire year leave with one-half salary. Faculty are usually eligible for a sabbatical leave every seven years and the competition for them is stiff. You may be able to help a faculty member do research during sabbatical. It may prove interesting to work elbow to elbow with a professor who has the time to be creative and informally teach you on a more personal level.

College Freshmen Ought to Know:

112. that the phrase **publish or perish** is commonly heard and usually true for faculty members, particularly in larger institutions where research is heavily promoted. Awards, Nobel prizes, grant money, all gain great notoriety for universities and these things are easily counted when comparing universities to each other. (But who's counting? To be honest, everybody!) The problem is that some research faculty may be poor teachers. Their lives revolve around their research or creative production and publishing, performing, or exhibiting is the way they get noticed, evaluated, and promoted in rank. However, the best professors blend it all together. This improves the quality of their teaching.

College Freshmen Ought to Know:

113. that the role of **part-time faculty** can be confusing. (Sometimes called **adjunct** faculty.)   In some cases they are hired simply as less costly instructors, with no need to pay medical and salary benefits — just flat fee per each credit hour taught. Some colleges can save a lot of money by hiring a large percentage of part-time faculty. The association that grants accreditation to the college will complain if the percent of part-time faculty gets too high; usually they don't like to see part-time faculty compose more than a third of any one depart-

ment. On the other hand, some part-time instructors are teaching because they love it and the college is able to take advantage of great knowledge and experience in the field that this person can bring to the classroom. Many part-time professionals fit this category: law, architecture, music, art, poetry, etc. As for quality instruction, it's just like for full-time faculty, you will get some marvelous instructors and you will get some terrible ones.

College Freshmen Ought to Know:

114. that when looking at the master schedule of courses offered for a term you will notice a number of courses being taught by **T.B.A.**, or **Staff**. This simply means that at the time the schedule was printed no staff member was yet assigned to the course. T.B.A. means "to be announced," usually by noticing who appears at the doorway when the class first meets. Sometimes not listing the instructor is done to prevent large numbers of students from either signing up for easy or good instructors and avoiding instructors with reputations as poor or too rigorous. Not surprisingly, students seem to know which instructors are important to experience and which are to be avoided at all cost.

College Freshmen Ought to Know:

115. that **T.A.** means teaching assistant. These people are usually graduate students majoring in the field in which they are teaching. T.A.'s are used a lot in larger universities so that faculty can teach fewer sessions of courses. This saves the college money that would be paid to faculty members and gives the T.A.'s teaching experience. T.A.'s might be responsible for sessions between major lectures by a professor or they may offer tutorials. Sometimes T.A.'s become a wall that protects faculty members from students. If you need to see the professor be politely persistent in setting up an appointment to talk. Remember that the entire system of higher education exists in order to educate you. Sometimes faculty need to be reminded of this.

College Freshmen Ought to Know:

116. that **tutors** are intended to serve all students. Good students who think tutors are intended to help only weak students often earn a D, which stands for DUMB FOR THAT THOUGHT. Many top students seek tutoring as a way to improve their understanding and often turn a C mid-term grade into an A or B final grade. Realize your need for a tutor as soon as possible. All of us have difficulty sometimes. Turn difficulty into opportunity. Get help. My advice: when

in trouble do everything, and I mean everything, to get yourself out of the trouble. Tutors can help show you the way. If your first tutor does not work out, ask for another. Their abilities are as varied as the students. Remember, you have the right to receive tutoring. But also remember that a tutor is there to help you become independent of them, not to do the work for you.

College Freshmen Ought to Know:

117. that **accreditation** is important to the college. Accreditation is a stamp of approval from an organization set up to measure colleges, universities, and even specialized fields of study within the colleges. Look near the front of the college catalog and see what national organization(s) approve the way the college operates. All aspects of the college get measured: student recruitment, retention, evaluation, faculty-student ratios, part-time to full-time faculty ratios, faculty evaluations and promotions, administrative procedures, goals and objectives of the colleges. The latest efforts are centered on measuring something called **outcomes assessment**. This is about looking for methods of measuring success of students after completing courses. Students think exams ought to clarify the relative success of students in a course, but the issue is a larger one. Outcomes assessment is

trying to measure if students really are achieving the goals and objectives of the courses — not just passing the exams. What if the exams really didn't measure what was taught? What if what was taught really was not a goal of the course? Students may get good grades without having experienced what they should have. Some faculty are not happy to participate in activities dealing with these issues because they say it takes time away from issues that really matter such as their research. Others, like state legislatures who must approve the spending of billions of tax dollars on education, are beginning to insist that something exist to measure the success or failure of spending that money. Outcomes assessment is a big issue in American education and you will be reading and hearing more about it.

STUDENT: "I WASN'T IN CLASS LAST TIME – DID I MISS ANYTHING?"
INSTRUCTOR: "OF COURSE NOT. ONCE I REALIZED YOU WEREN'T HERE I CANCELLED CLASSES UNTIL YOU COULD MAKE IT!"

Student Rights and Responsibilities

Understanding and respecting your rights
and the rights of others

College Freshmen Ought to Know:

118. that students *and* faculty are expected to **understand basic legal rights and responsibilities** regarding individuals as students and as educators. Faculty will be held accountable for reasonable actions and are expected to exercise sound judgement in their role as educators. Students considering certain actions or activities ought to think about what would be a reasonable and customary response to what they are contemplating. How will this action be received? What is the intent? How much attention do you want to attract? Are you acting alone or with a large group? Actions involv-

ing protest of some sort must be carefully considered for maximum effectiveness — not just emotional roller-coasters. Articles in the student newspapers, particular art exhibits, invitations to controversial speakers, as well as protest actions all have potential for causing clashes with authorities and with fellow students. It is important to remember that just because individuals have become students or faculty members, they have not relinquished their rights to due process in the justice system beyond the campus.

College Freshmen Ought to Know:

119. that there is a **student body constitution** that among other things lists the rights and responsibilities of students. Make sure you have a copy and skim through enough of it to know what kinds of activities are listed and how certain behavior is handled.

College Freshmen Ought to Know:

120. that **students are responsible** for their own lives. You must have your own reasons for doing and becoming what you are. You will be expected to possess, and to use **common sense** in dealing with individual situations. No two situations are ever exactly the same. Knowing how to take care of yourself and striving to achieve what's important to you will propel you far in college. Others: parents, friends, can tell you what you ought to do, where you ought to go, or whatever, but it will never work out unless you have decided that it is what you want for yourself. Sometimes it takes people years to figure this out — some never do understand and they lead lives of wondering without ever accomplishing satisfaction for themselves.

SINKING SOUNDS:

A. I THOUGHT THE EXAM WAS NEXT TIME.

B. DO YOU HAVE A PENCIL I CAN USE?

C. WHEN IS THE LAST DAY TO WITHDRAW FROM A COURSE?

Time Line

**Understanding where you're going,
what you'll need to get there, and when**

121. Be selfish for a minute. Take some time for yourself and list all the important things you want out of your life. These are your goals. Use a separate sheet of paper for practice, then transfer your well-thought-out goals on the pages following. List things you absolutely must have, things it would be nice to have, list things you absolutely don't want . List things you want to do and things you want to avoid doing. Rank order them: #1, #2, #3, and so on. Next, list in a second column what you must do to achieve what you want and to avoid what you don't want. Of course your mind will change about things, but it's important to go through the process of writing out a list. It helps establish priorities in working towards goals.

Once you have a list of goals, place them on the time line about where you expect them to appear in your lifetime. With the goals written down, think about what has to happen in order to make the goal a reality. Now, write down those things necessary and place them in the necessary sequence. What has to happen first? And so on.

Be honest. Think about what's important and what's not. If you can't write out some kind of list of goals, you are going through life like a billiard ball just waiting for something to happen to you. Is that any way to live your own life?

Birth

_____

_____

_____

_____

_____

_____

_____

_____

_____

_____

_____

_____

Death

Time Line Summary

No doubt you found this exercise difficult, challenging, worrisome, and filled with uncertanties. Yet your experience is a lesson for life. People don't get places unless they know where they're going, what they'll need to get there, and have some time frame in mind. Time lines help give you direction. As you've probably discovered, doing one as a road map for life is difficult. However, it's a worthwhile exercise for two reasons. First, it gives you experience with something successful people have learned to do well. Second, once done on something as awesome and uncertain as your future life, realize how much easier it can be when applied towards something smaller like a college course. It's time management personalized. Working on and through those time lines will aid you in being successful in college and life. People you consider heros or models in your life probably have some kind of time line reference for their lives. It was difficult for them as well as you. Re-visit this exercise after you've talked with others about your ideas. Do some more thinking. Plot what you decide. That way this exercise will be less 'something you *have* to do' and more 'something you'll *want* to do.' Welcome to the start of your future travels.

Conclusion

You've finished. Or have you just begun? A lot was covered in a few short hours of reading. Understand that reading is not always retaining information. To do that, you usually have to use the information in some meaningful way. Think about that. Re-read relevant parts of *100 Things* and write down your reactions. Think about what you'll do with the information and who else you may want to talk with about certain topics. Then see if you can get other students energized to discuss and give their perspectives about interesting topics. The final entry of the Time Line is a perfect example of an open ended discussion.

An interesting thing happens when you learn the value of interacting with and discussing information, confusing points, or difficult concepts with others — you find yourself listening and learning more easily than on your own.

Networking, interacting with people, and discussing issues is a tremendous way to learn and get things done. These topics will help you get the most out of your freshman year. However, it's all up to you. Talk to others, see if you can begin to put things in a wider context. Take an argumentative viewpoint and see if you can defend it. Cooperate and see if you can find a learning partner to help ease your way.

These are valuable methods. You have the choices as to how to learn about college and how to learn about its importance in your life.

Reading about those choices, interacting with specific and meaningful topics, and then discussing them with others can help you make those choices more easily and intelligently. Start practicing this method now and see how easy it becomes to learn from similar discussions about college textbooks you read or lectures you hear.

Final Note to Contributing Editors (students, faculty, staff, parents)

Your insights are valuable. I'd appreciate your ideas to help next year's students. Please take a moment and share with me things you'd like included in the next edition. A form is provided on the next few pages for this purpose. I'd also appreciate any critical comment about what is good and what should be changed. Thank you.

Editorial Comments and Contribution Pages

Dear Reader,

Your comments can help the next incoming freshman class to make a smoother transition to college. Please share your thoughts, ideas, and suggestions on the following pages or on a separate sheet of paper. Also, fill in the biographical information below. I'll include a special reference by-line in my next edition to acknowledge all contributors. Thank you!

Name _____   ☐ *Student*
                                                          ☐ *Faculty*
Institution _____   ☐ *Administrator*
                                                          ☐ *Parent*
City _____ State _____ Zip _____   ☐ _____

(Cut or tear out form)

My thoughts, ideas, and suggestions are

_____
_____
_____
_____
_____
_____
_____
_____
_____
_____
_____
_____

(Cut or tear out form)

_____

_____

_____

_____

_____

_____

_____

_____

Mail To: Professor William Disbro
            c/o The Cambridge Stratford Study Skills Institute
            8560 Main Street
            Williamsville, NY 14221

(Cut or tear out form)

Pre-requisite times credit hour minus imputed equals . . .

Appendix

**Campus Services, Interesting Statistics,
Works Consulted, Index,
About the Publisher**

Your Most Valuable Appendix is Your Official College Catalog

Understand that though it's sometimes difficult to read and digest the official college catalog at the beginning, its use is invaluable and **it should not be overlooked**. It should be reviewed soon after you finish *100 Things*.

Colleges and universities are quite different and many offer specific services, course options, degree requirements, and special experiences that are outlined in the catalog. With the information you've gained from *100 Things*, you can begin to research many of the areas of greatest interest. Highlight sections that are most appropriate and be sure to ask questions of your advisor, your instructors, and your fellow students. The new understanding that results will make your college catalog relevant in guiding you throughout your college experience, and will help make your dream of that cap and gown on graduation day a reality.

Campus Services

Student Service Professionals can be invaluable in helping you succeed. Listed below are brief descriptions of a few such services. Following these descriptions is a list of typical student services that exist on college campuses. Check those that are available at your college and list their locations for future reference.

Counseling centers provide aptitude and interest testing to help you decide what field to major in if you are unsure. They give you information about what is required in different fields. Counselors also work with students who have personal or family problems or problems involving educational or career planning, etc.

Placement centers can give you up-to-date information about career opportunities, help you get part-time or summer jobs while in college, and place you in appropriate positions when you graduate. Also, they usually have information about entrance requirements for graduate and professional programs and catalogs of other colleges.

Learning center staff can diagnose your learning problems and provide special help in reading, problem solving skills, preparing for exams, test taking skills, reducing test anxiety, etc. They can help find trained tutors as well, and often have computer labs or can direct you to where you can get computer assisted instruction in basic skills or in a specialized subject.

Almost all colleges have **writing centers** with instructors and tutors who are specially trained in helping students improve their writing.

Math labs are usually available if you are having problems in math. In some colleges, math labs are part of the math department; in others they are part of the learning center or are independent.

Student Services	Check if Available	List the Location
Learning Assistance Center		
Writing Center		
Math Lab		
Tutoring Center		
Counseling Center		
Student Health Clinic		
Job Placement Office		
Student Activities Office		
Student Government Office		
Campus Chapels		
Child Care Centers		

Student Services	Check if Available	List the Location
Academic Advisement Center	_____	_____
Art, Music, Theater Centers	_____	_____
Athletic Centers	_____	_____
Residence Life Center	_____	_____
Campus Security Office	_____	_____
Commuter Services Office	_____	_____

Now that you know what campus services are available, do you know what services they offer? **No?** Check your college catalog, pick up a brochure describing campus services, or **"boldly go where no freshman has gone before"** . . . stop by the office, introduce yourself, and ASK. Successful students usually know about these services long before they need them.

Interesting Educational Statistics

I've included the following education statistics because you may find them interesting and beneficial. They can give a wider prespective on who and where you are in the bigger context of education nationally.

All statistics from: U.S. Bureau of the Census, Statistical Abstract of the United States: 1994 (114th edition). Washington, DC 1994

College Enrollment by Sex

	Male	Female
1960	2.3 mil	1.2 mil
1992	6.2	7.8

Persons 25 years and over completing college

1970	11%
1993	22%

Educational Attainment, by Race and Ethnicity
Completed 4 Years of College or More

	Total	White	Black	Hispanic
1960	7.7%	8.1%	3.1%	NA
1993	21.9%	22.6%	12.2%	9.0%

Scholastic Aptitude Test (SAT) Scores of College-Bound Seniors

	1967	1993
Verbal, total points	466	424
Math, total points	492	478

College Freshman – Summary Characteristics:
(First-time full-time freshmen 1993)

% of Freshmen class:

37% applied to three or more colleges

27% received average grade in high school of A– to A+

57% received average grade in high school of B– to B+

16% received average grade in high school of C to C+

Probable field of study

8% Arts and Humanities

16% Business

3% Physical science

20% Professional

2% Computer science

6% Biological sciences

10% Education

9% Engineering

9% Social science

3% Technical

2% Communication

Political Orientation
- 25%   Liberal
- 50%   Middle of the road
- 21%   Conservative

Attitudes – agree or strongly agree
- 24%   activities of married women are best confined to home and family
- 22%   capital punishment should be abolished
- 28%   legalize marijuana
- 68%   there is too much concern for the rights of criminals
- 62%   abortion should be legal
- 65%   aspire to an advanced degree

Years Spent Earning Bachelor's Degree 1990
(% of all persons earning degree)

4 years or less	43.2%
5 years or less	65.3%
6 years or less	74.0%

Number of Higher Education Institutions

1970	2,556
1992 prel.	3,638

Total Higher Education Enrollment

1970	8,581,000
1992 prel.	14,491,000

Higher Education Degrees Conferred 1990

Associate's	482,000
Bachelor's	1,095,000
Master's	337,000
Doctorate's	39,000
First-professional	72,000

Number of Colleges in Selected States

Alaska	8	New Hampshire	29
California	322	New York	320
Illinois	169	Ohio	165
Massachusetts	117	Texas	176

Major Federal Student Financial Assistance Programs

	1980	1993 est.
Pell Grant recipients	$2,708,000	$4,300,000
Perkins Loan funds utilized	$694,000,000	$720,000,000
Stafford Loan funds utilized	$6,200,000	$16,425,000

Average College Costs for Undergraduates 1993-94

	Public	Private
4-Year College, total	$8,562.00	$17,846.00

Selected Salary Offers to Candidates for Bachelor's Degrees 1993

Accounting	$27,493.	Physics	$31,480.
Business, general	$24,555.	Social Sciences	$22,684.
Chemical Engineering	$39,482.	Humanities	$24,373.

Works Consulted

Bonjean, Charles M. "Social Science." *The World Book Encyclopedia*. 1990 ed.

Cambron-McCabe, Nelda H., and Martha M. McCarthy. Public School Law: Teachers' and Students' Rights. 3rd ed. Boston: Allyn and Bacon, 1992.

Crawford, June J. *Ten Tips for Academic Success*. 3rd ed. New York: Cambridge Stratford, Ltd., 1994.

Ellis, David. *Becoming a Master Student*. 7th ed. Boston: Houghton Mifflin, 1994.

Estell, Doug, Michele L. Satchwell, and Patricia S. Wright. *Reading Lists for College-Bound Students*. 2nd ed. New York: Prentice Hall (ARCO), 1993.

Flowers, Betty Sue, ed. *Joseph Campbell The Power of Myth with Bill Moyers.* New York: Doubleday, 1988.

Gross, Richard E. "Social Science." *Encyclopedia Americana.* 1988 ed.

Lockmiller, David A. "Degrees, Academic." *The Encyclopedia of Education.* 1971 ed.

MacDonald, Ross B. *Becoming a Master Tutor: A Guidebook for More Effective Tutoring.* 1st ed. New York: Cambridge Stratford, Ltd., 1994.

McPherson, Bruce. "humanities, education in the." *Academic American Encyclopedia.* 1988 ed.

U.S. Bureau of the Census, Statistical Abstract of the United States: 1994 (114th edition). Washington, DC 1994.

Index by Item Number

About the Publisher
The Cambridge Stratford Study Skills Institute

Cambridge Stratford, Ltd. formed The Cambridge Stratford Study Skills Institute in 1985 with the help of its current president, Peter W. Stevens, a former vice president from a private college in New York. It is an international organization of learning and study skills specialists and tutor training professionals dedicated to helping students of all ages to STUDY SMARTER, READ FASTER and SCORE HIGHER ON TESTS, key ingredients for success in school as well as in life.

Cambridge Stratford Study Skills Course System

The CSSS INSTITUTE provides teacher and tutor training services, private courses for students in summer and after school programs nationally, and publishes the internationally renowned study skills curriculum entitled **The Cambridge Stratford Study Skills Course**. It is taught publicly by schools, colleges, federal and state grant programs at 3 levels (6–8th: 20 hour edition, 9–11th: 30 hour edition, and 12–15th: 10 hour edition, entitled *Ten Tips for Academic Success*, available in English and Spanish). These editions include 4 components; Student Workbook, Teacher Manual, Transparency and Listening Tape Set.

Tutor Training Research Study

In 1994, The INSTITUTE introduced a research-based tutor training curriculum nationally under the direction of Dr. Ross MacDonald entitled *The Master Tutor: A Guidebook for More Effective Tutoring*. It includes the state-of-the-art methods tutors can use to improve one-on-one tutoring sessions and consists of a self-instructional Guidebook for tutors, a Tutor Trainer's Manual, and Transparency Set.

Improving the Retention of College Students

The CSSS INSTITUTE's mission is to help students prepare for and succeed in college. This newest book, *100 Things Every College Freshman Ought to Know*, represents its further effort to help college-bound students adjust to the difficult transition required in becoming a college freshman. It is a suggested reading for high school seniors, entering college freshmen, or anyone who is returning to school after a time lapse in their education (i.e., adult education). Colleges may find it helpful in their retention-management efforts since it helps new students learn the vocabulary and college environment in order to understand the college catalog. Plus, it offers valuable information on customs, behaviors, and practices that can increase college success.

If you need information about any of the products or services offered or would like a sample lesson (PREVIEW MANUAL) forwarded for your review, write or call today.

NOTE: Prospective Authors — *100 Things* is being planned as a series. If you have an idea, book, or concept that might help students succeed in school or college, please contact us. We're interested!

The Cambridge Stratford Study Skills Institute
8560 Main Street
Williamsville, New York 14221
(716) 626-9044 or FAX (716) 626-9076

The
Cambridge
Stratford
Study Skills
Institute™

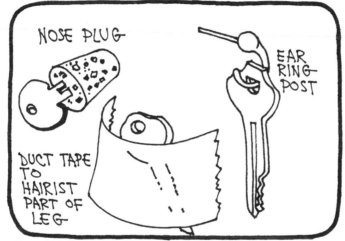

Interesting solutions to not losing dorm key.

Communication Stick-Ups
(Cut out and use as messages for friends, roommates.)

"I don't need the computer, I'm just standing here meditating."

"Is the washing machine broken or are you conducting an experiment?"

"I'm probably not, but if I am, DON'T BREATHE!

Communication Stick-Ups
(Cut out and use as messages for friends, roommates.)

"Cleanliness is a virtue."

"Talk to me in the morning."

"If, at first, you fail . . ."

"This book provides a pleasant, painless, and practical way to introduce freshmen to the customs and mores of college life. It describes what we should know before we start college, but too often learn later the hard way.

Martha Maxwell
Learning Assistance Expert/Author/Consultant

"This book serves to open the eyes of high school seniors to that world beyond called college. It covers the key differences students must adjust to in furthering their education beyond high school and serves as an ideal orientation to the customs, practices, vocabulary, and procedures used by colleges. High school guidance counselors should recommend **100 Things** *on their suggested reading lists for college-bound students."*

Dr. Jan Mickler
Supervisor of Language Arts
Division of Teaching, Learning, and Student Services
Chattanooga Public Schools

*"From the educator's perspective, this is an excellent primer to one's first term of college in that it bridges the time between entry to higher education and the crucial first six (6) weeks — the time in which one must adjust to a new world of learning. This self tutorial in its bullet approach is enlightening and informative with respect to answering the "who," "what," "where," "why," and "so what" significance of college. **Retention, success and graduation** are the goals of higher education's "permanent" residents. This book meets these needs and more! I encourage its use by both academic and student service providers and would have recommended it to my own college-age children."*

Dr. Phillip Santa Maria
Associate Vice President and Dean of Students
State University College at Buffalo